INSIDE THE NFL

TENNESSEE TITANS

BY WILLIAM MEIER

SportsZone
An Imprint of Abdo Publishing
abdobooks.com

abdobooks.com

Published by Abdo Publishing, a division of ABDO, PO Box 398166, Minneapolis, Minnesota 55439.

Printed in the United States of America, North Mankato, Minnesota
042019
092019

THIS BOOK CONTAINS
RECYCLED MATERIALS

Cover Photo: Ryan Kang/AP Images
Interior Photos: Wade Payne/AP Images, 5; Al Messerschmidt/AP Images, 6; Scott Audette/AP Images, 8; Tom Hauck/Getty Images Sport/Getty Images, 11; NFL Photos/AP Images, 13, 15, 21, 26; AP Images, 17, 22, 25, 43; Ed Kolenovsky/AP Images, 19; Tom DiPace/AP Images, 29; Stephen Dunn/Allsport/Getty Images Sport/Getty Images, 31; Mark Humphrey/AP Images, 33; Randy Piland/The Tennessean/AP Images, 34; Amy Sancetta/AP Images, 37; Wesley Hitt/AP Images, 40

Editor: Patrick Donnelly
Series Designer: Craig Hinton

Library of Congress Control Number: 2018966004

Publisher's Cataloging-in-Publication Data

Names: Meier, William, author.
Title: Tennessee Titans / by William Meier
Description: Minneapolis, Minnesota: Abdo Publishing, 2020 | Series: Inside the NFL | Includes online resources and index.
Identifiers: ISBN 9781532118661 (lib. bdg.) | ISBN 9781532172847 (ebook)
Subjects: LCSH: Tennessee Titans (Football team)--Juvenile literature. | National Football League--Juvenile literature. | Football teams--Juvenile literature. | American football--Juvenile literature.
Classification: DDC 796.33264--dc23

TABLE OF CONTENTS

CHAPTER 1

MUSIC CITY MIRACLE

The Tennessee Titans' playoff victory over the Buffalo Bills on January 8, 2000, was one that had to be seen to be believed. To this day, it is called a "miracle."

The Titans trailed the Bills 16–15 in an American Football Conference (AFC) wild-card game at Adelphia Coliseum in Nashville, Tennessee. Buffalo's Steve Christie had just kicked a 41-yard field goal. Only 16 seconds remained in the game. Tennessee's season appeared to be ending.

To win, the Titans needed to either return Buffalo's kickoff for a touchdown or take it back deep enough into Bills territory to set up a field-goal attempt. It is difficult to make those kinds of kickoff returns in the National Football League (NFL). The Titans' chances appeared slim.

Tennessee's Kevin Dyson heads down the sideline against Buffalo in their January 2000 playoff game.

TITANS
87

As Benji Olson (75) and Frank Wycheck (89) look on, the officials discuss whether Wycheck's lateral was legal.

However, Tennessee had been practicing a surprise play. It was the Titans' only shot at winning. And amazingly, it worked.

Christie kicked off to the Titans. Lorenzo Neal fielded the ball at the Tennessee 25-yard line and handed it to teammate Frank Wycheck. The Bills' coverage team chased Wycheck toward the right sideline. Then Wycheck stopped, turned, and threw the ball overhand back across the field to Kevin Dyson. Dyson caught the lateral, or backward pass, and headed down the left sideline. A wall of blockers stood between him and the stunned Buffalo players. The Bills tried to recover and get back across the field. They could not get there in time.

Dyson finished his 75-yard dash to the end zone with three seconds left. The play was reviewed on video by the officials. It was legal for Wycheck to throw the ball overhand across the field as long as the pass did not go forward. Forward passes are illegal on kickoff returns. Although the replay showed that the play was close, officials ruled it was legal. The crowd at Adelphia Coliseum went wild. The Bills could not repeat the Titans' kickoff feat on the game's last play. Tennessee won 22–16.

"We believe in miracles," Titans safety Blaine Bishop said. "This is something special. It's unbelievable."

CRASH COURSE

The Titans had practiced the play they called "Home Run Throwback" approximately 60 times during the 1999 season. It was the play the team used to pull off the shocking win over Buffalo. Kevin Dyson was never part of the practice. But when the Titans used the play for the only time in a game, Dyson stepped into the starring role.

The way the play was designed, kick returner Derrick Mason was supposed to receive the lateral pass. Mason, however, was out injured with a concussion. Anthony Dorsett, who had gotten some practice as Mason's backup, had leg cramps. Coaches called for Dyson, a wide receiver, to fill in.

"As we were running on the field, they were trying to explain . . . the play," Dyson said of his teammates.

Dyson figured it out just in time to score one of the most famous touchdowns in NFL history.

Running back Eddie George fights for extra yardage in Tennessee's 33–14 AFC title-game win over Jacksonville on January 23, 2000.

The play became known as "the Music City Miracle." The Titans' home city of Nashville is called "Music City" because it is the headquarters for the country music industry.

The 1999 season was just the Titans' third season in Tennessee and second in Nashville. The team originally played in Houston and was called the Oilers. The Oilers moved to

Memphis, Tennessee, for the 1997 season. In 1999 the team changed its name from Oilers to Titans and moved into the brand-new Adelphia Coliseum, its third home stadium in three seasons in its new state.

After the Music City Miracle, the Titans won their next two playoff games, too. They beat the Indianapolis Colts and Jacksonville Jaguars on the road. The win over the Jaguars came in the AFC Championship Game. It put the Titans in the Super Bowl for the first time in the franchise's 40 seasons.

Like the Music City Miracle, Super Bowl XXXIV would also feature one of the most exciting finishes in NFL history. The Titans faced the St. Louis Rams in Atlanta. Quarterback Steve McNair and running back Eddie George led Tennessee's strong offense. But the Rams were the highest-scoring team in the NFL. They would be tough to stop.

Indeed, St. Louis quarterback Kurt Warner played well. He set a

AFC CHAMPIONS

The Titans became AFC champions for the first time by following up the 22–16 victory over the Bills with two more playoff wins. Tennessee topped Indianapolis 19–16 and Jacksonville 33–14. Eddie George rushed for 162 yards against the Colts. Against the Jaguars, the Titans trailed 14–10 at halftime but outscored Jacksonville 23–0 in the second half.

Super Bowl record with 414 passing yards. The Rams jumped to a 16-point lead. George began chipping away at it with two rushing touchdowns. The Titans tied the score at 16 on a 43-yard field goal by Al Del Greco with 2:12 left in the game.

But the Rams came right back. Warner threw a 73-yard touchdown pass to Isaac Bruce on their next offensive play. That put St. Louis ahead 23–16 with 1:54 to play. Like so many games in Tennessee's thrilling 1999 season, this one would come down to the final seconds. In this case, it came down to the final play and the final yard.

A penalty on the kickoff return pinned the Titans at their own 10-yard line. But McNair quickly marched them down the field. They reached the Rams' 10-yard line with five seconds to play. They had time for one last play.

The Rams flooded the end zone with defenders to prevent a touchdown pass. Instead of throwing into coverage, McNair found Dyson on the move just inside the 5-yard line. Dyson caught the ball and headed for the end zone. Mike Jones had other ideas. The Rams linebacker grabbed Dyson and pulled him to the ground. Dyson desperately reached the ball out. But he fell less than a yard short of the end zone as time ran out.

Dyson comes up inches short of the end zone on the last play of the Titans' 23–16 defeat in Super Bowl XXXIV.

The game is considered by many football experts and fans to be one of the best Super Bowls ever. The loss was difficult for the Titans to accept, however.

"To come this far and be a half-yard short is just a sick feeling," Dyson said. "When he got his hands on me, I thought I'd break the tackle. But he . . . made a great play."

Although the Titans fell less than a yard short, the season was the team's best in the NFL. The franchise began in the American Football League (AFL) in 1960. Although they had made only one Super Bowl appearance through the 2018 season, they'd had plenty of exciting moments and colorful players along the way.

CHAPTER 2

NEW TEAM, LEAGUE, AND CHAMPION

George Blanda did not play football in 1959. At 32 years old, he had retired from the Chicago Bears of the NFL.

Blanda was settling into a new job as a sales manager for a trucking company. Meanwhile, a Texas oilman named K. S. "Bud" Adams Jr. was working to get into professional football. Adams was unable to buy his way into the NFL. So instead he turned his focus to the new AFL, which was established to compete with the NFL. His Houston Oilers were one of eight teams to play in 1960 as original AFL members.

The AFL presented a new opportunity for hundreds of football players around the country. Blanda was back on the field with the Oilers in 1960, and his comeback was a

Quarterback George Blanda returned to football in 1960 with the Houston Oilers. He led them to the AFL's first two titles.

16

big success. On New Year's Day 1961, he had a chance to lead his new team to victory in the first AFL Championship Game.

In the fourth quarter, the Oilers were clinging to a 17–16 lead over the Los Angeles Chargers. Houston was backed up to its 12-yard line. Blanda could have played it safe. But that was not his style. And it certainly was not the style of the new league trying to make an impression on the nation's fans. Sensing a blitz, Blanda flipped a pass to Billy Cannon. The Oilers' star running back broke a tackle and took off. He didn't stop until he reached the end zone. The 88-yard touchdown pass closed the scoring in Houston's 24–16 victory.

Cannon caught three passes for 128 yards. He also returned three kickoffs for 81 yards and rushed for 50 yards. He earned Most Valuable Player (MVP) honors for the first AFL Championship Game. Blanda passed for 301 yards and three touchdowns. And he booted a field goal and three extra points in his role as the Oilers' kicker.

BUD ADAMS

Bud Adams, the founder of the Oilers, owned the Oilers/Tennessee Titans team until his death in 2013. Adams was a native of Bartlesville, Oklahoma. He played football at the Culver Military Academy, Menlo College in California, and the University of Kansas. After serving in the Navy during World War II, Adams started an oil company in Houston in 1946. He became one of the original AFL team owners in 1959.

Billy Cannon runs against the Dallas Texans in the 1962 AFL Championship Game.

The Oilers were just getting started. After the team began the 1961 season with a 1–3–1 record, the offense started to roll. They were riding a six-game winning streak when the undefeated Chargers, by then playing in San Diego, visited Houston on December 3 for a rematch of the championship game. Blanda threw four touchdown passes and kicked a league-record 55-yard field goal as the Oilers beat the Chargers 33–13. Blanda was named the AFL Player of the Year. The Oilers scored an average of 36.6 points per game.

On Christmas Eve 1961, Cannon earned his second straight AFL Championship Game MVP award. He caught five passes in the game. One was a 35-yarder in the third quarter for a touchdown. The Oilers beat the Chargers 10–3.

Houston won its third straight AFL East Division title with an 11–3 mark in 1962. The Oilers went back to the AFL Championship Game. They rallied to erase a 17-point halftime deficit only to lose 20–17 in two overtimes to the Dallas Texans.

GEORGE BLANDA

George Blanda's career lasted 26 seasons as a quarterback and place kicker, a record for professional football. His most successful seasons as a quarterback came with the Oilers in the early days of the AFL. Blanda was the AFL Player of the Year in 1961. That season, he led Houston to a second straight AFL championship.

Blanda might have gained his greatest fame, however, with the Oakland Raiders in 1970. That season, Blanda led the Raiders to five straight comeback wins or ties. Blanda was 43 years old at that time. In his career, Blanda scored 2,002 points—all but 54 as a kicker—and had a hand in 1,416 more by throwing 236 touchdown passes.

He played 10 seasons for the Chicago Bears, from 1949 to 1958. Blanda retired for one season. Then he came back in 1960 with Houston. He played for the Oilers for their first seven seasons. He then played nine more with the Raiders. He retired from the NFL in 1975 at the age of 48.

Blanda throws a pass to fullback Charley Tolar in a 1965 game against the New York Jets.

The team Adams created was off to an incredible start. But there would be no additional league titles to celebrate in the decades ahead. Houston slipped to 6–8 in 1963. The Oilers had just one more winning season in the AFL. They went 9–4–1 in 1967. A 6–6–2 record in 1969 was enough to get Houston into the playoffs as the second-place team in the Eastern Division. Their last game as an AFL member, however, ended in disappointment. Daryle Lamonica threw six touchdown passes to lead the Oakland Raiders to a 56–7 rout over Houston in an AFL semifinal.

CHAPTER 3

KNOCKING AT THE DOOR

Few people saw the AFL as a threat to the NFL when it kicked off in 1960. But it wasn't long before the NFL took its new rival seriously. The leagues announced a merger in June 1966. The Oilers and the nine other AFL teams became part of the NFL through a merger in 1970.

The Oilers went through more schedule changes than any other AFL team. They had been in the AFL East with the New York Jets, Boston Patriots, Buffalo Bills, and Miami Dolphins. They were placed in the AFC Central Division when they joined the NFL. The other teams in the Central were the Cincinnati Bengals, Pittsburgh Steelers, and Cleveland Browns. Cincinnati came from the AFL West. Pittsburgh and Cleveland were two of the three teams that moved over

Oilers defensive end Elvin Bethea chases after Cowboys quarterback Roger Staubach in a 1970 exhibition game.

ELVIN BETHEA

Elvin Bethea provided longevity and excellence at the defensive end position for Houston. He came to the Oilers as a third-round draft pick out of North Carolina A&T in 1968. Bethea set team records for most seasons (16), consecutive games played (135), and total games played (210). He had 105 sacks when it was an unofficial statistic. That total would stand as a team record if it were recognized as official.

from the original NFL to balance the conferences.

Before the first NFL season in 1970, Houston grabbed some Texas bragging rights. Wide receiver Jerry LeVias scored three touchdowns for the Oilers in their 37–21 exhibition game victory over the Dallas Cowboys. Houston started the regular season 2–1. But it won just one more game and finished last in the AFC Central with a 3–10–1 record.

The Oilers escaped last place for the only time in their first four NFL seasons when they won the final three games of the 1971 season to finish 4–9–1. That was miles ahead of their performance the next two seasons, when they were 1–13 in each.

The turnaround began in 1974 when the Oilers went 7–7, their best record since 1968. Colorful coach O. A. "Bum" Phillips joined the staff for that season as defensive coordinator under veteran coach Sid Gillman. Phillips took over as head coach

Dan Pastorini was the Oilers' starting quarterback throughout most of the 1970s.

the next season. The improvement continued. The Oilers' 10–4 record in 1975 was the team's best since 1962.

In 1977 they took over the AFC Central lead in the fourth week with a 27–10 win over Pittsburgh. But Houston played

✕ It usually took more than one defender to bring down Earl Campbell.

two games without starting quarterback Dan Pastorini and five without future Hall of Fame defensive end Elvin Bethea because of injuries. The Oilers settled for an 8–6 record. But the team believed it was on the verge of becoming a playoff squad.

Beginning in 1978, Phillips led the Oilers to three straight playoff appearances. In the process, he captured the city of Houston's imagination with his trademark cowboy hat and colorful quips. He also had help from rookie running back Earl Campbell, who led the NFL with 1,450 rushing yards and scored 13 touchdowns.

The 1978 team finished 10–6, then pulled off playoff upsets at Miami and New England to reach the AFC Championship Game. The ride ended there, however, as the Oilers ran into the Pittsburgh Steelers, who were in the midst of winning four Super Bowls in six seasons in the 1970s. The Steelers' emphatic 34–5 victory showed the Oilers they still had work to do.

Houston clinched its return to the playoffs in 1979 with a 20–17 win over Pittsburgh. The Oilers went 11–5 and Campbell won the NFL's MVP Award. He led the league with 1,679 rushing yards and 19 touchdowns.

EARL CAMPBELL

Earl Campbell was a 5-foot-11, 232-pound wrecking ball of a running back. He had won the 1977 Heisman Trophy at the University of Texas. Then he lived up to expectations after he was the first player taken in the 1978 NFL Draft. Campbell led the NFL in rushing in each of his first three seasons and made the Pro Bowl in five of his first six years.

Known for pummeling defenders, Campbell also took a pounding throughout his career. He spent his final season and a half with the New Orleans Saints. That completed a career that lasted eight years and produced 9,407 rushing yards and 74 rushing touchdowns. Campbell was inducted into the Pro Football Hall of Fame in 1991.

Of the three playoff teams of that era, Oilers fans were most excited by the 1979 squad. The offense was slowed by injuries. But Houston did not stop. The Oilers won two playoff games, including a 17–14 road upset of the San Diego Chargers. Houston advanced to a second straight AFC Championship Game matchup with the mighty Steelers.

This time, on January 6, 1980, the Oilers played better. But a controversial call kept wide receiver Mike Renfro from scoring the tying touchdown late in the third quarter. The Oilers fell again to the Steelers, 27–13.

Despite their second straight AFC Championship Game loss to the Steelers, Oilers fans were impressed. When the team arrived home in Houston in the middle of the night, a crowd of approximately 70,000 was waiting at the Astrodome.

PLAYOFF PATH

Some special efforts were needed along the way to get the Oilers into the playoffs in 1978. Houston stopped Pittsburgh's perfect start at 7–0 by posting its first *Monday Night Football* win, 24–17, on October 23. Three weeks later, the Oilers trailed 23–0 before rallying to beat New England 26–23. Finally, after scoring three touchdowns against the Steelers, rookie running back Earl Campbell added four more on November 20 in a memorable Monday night victory over the Miami Dolphins, 35–30.

Oilers quarterback Ken Stabler and head coach Bum Phillips are dejected after losing to the Oakland Raiders in the 1980 playoffs.

The Oilers made it back to the playoffs the next season under a new quarterback. Former Raiders star Ken Stabler took over for Pastorini, and Campbell just kept getting better. The third-year pro rushed for 1,934 yards. At the time, it was the second-highest single-season rushing total in NFL history. But after a 27–7 first-round loss to the Oakland Raiders on December 28, 1980, owner Bud Adams fired Phillips.

The coaching change did not work. Houston suffered through six straight losing seasons. The Oilers fared as poorly

Longtime Oilers offensive guard Mike Munchak was inducted into the Pro Football Hall of Fame in 2001.

as 1–8 in the strike-shortened 1982 season and 2–14 in 1983. But those struggles resulted in high draft picks, and Houston cashed in by selecting offensive linemen in the first round for three straight years.

The Oilers added future Hall of Fame guards Mike Munchak in 1982 and Bruce Matthews in 1983. The next year they selected Dean Steinkuhler and moved him from guard to tackle. Then, when former Canadian Football League (CFL) star quarterback Warren Moon became available as a free agent, the Oilers outbid other NFL teams.

The Oilers team that took the field for the 1984 season featured Moon as its dynamic new quarterback. He played behind what was developing into a powerful offensive line. Both, however, needed time to figure out how to succeed in the NFL. By the end of the 1986 season, the passing game was taking shape. Moon threw for 3,489 yards. Drew Hill and Ernest Givins both went over 1,000 receiving yards.

The Oilers were ready to challenge their rivals again in 1987. They beat the Steelers 23–3 at Three Rivers Stadium in Pittsburgh. It was Houston's first win there since 1978. The Oilers went on to start a new streak of seven straight postseason appearances.

CHAPTER 4

LAST HURRAH IN HOUSTON

Warren Moon continued to lead the way for the Oilers in 1991. They won their first outright AFC Central Division championship that year. They clinched the title with a 31–6 win over Pittsburgh. In that game, Moon became the third quarterback in NFL history to pass for 4,000 yards in consecutive seasons. The team's division success continued in 1993, when the Oilers swept their Central foes and clinched the division title with a victory over the Steelers, this time 26–17 in Pittsburgh.

The Oilers were the only NFL team to make the playoffs each year from 1987 to 1993. It was a remarkable run. But Houston did not fare particularly well once it got into

Warren Moon started at quarterback for the Oilers from 1984 to 1993, leading them to seven playoff appearances.

the playoffs. It went 3–7 in that stretch and did not reach the AFC Championship Game.

Houston suffered some heartbreaking losses during that time. One came when quarterback John Elway rallied the Denver Broncos to a last-second 26–24 victory over the visiting Oilers on January 4, 1992. The most infamous loss, though, was Houston's 41–38 defeat to the host Buffalo Bills on January 3, 1993. The Oilers fell victim to the biggest comeback in NFL playoff history. They let a 35–3 lead get away in the wild-card game. Moon threw for 371 yards and four touchdowns in the loss.

WARREN MOON

When he didn't draw much interest from the NFL coming out of college in 1978, Warren Moon headed north to the CFL. There, he led the Edmonton Eskimos to a record five straight championships before returning to the United States in 1984. He still wound up retiring with the third-highest passing yardage and fourth-highest touchdown pass total in NFL history.

Houston made the most of Moon's combination of arm strength and mobility. He then went on to Minnesota, Seattle, and Kansas City late in his career.

Those playoff woes continued in 1993. Houston finished the regular season with a 24–0 shutout of the New York Jets. The Oilers became the fifth team in NFL history to finish a season with 11 straight wins. They also won 12 games for

Jeff Fisher made the move with the team to Tennessee in 1997. He remained coach through 2010.

the first time in team history. Unfortunately for Houston, the Kansas City Chiefs came to town and beat the Oilers 28–20 in the wild-card round of the playoffs.

The team went through a lot of turnover that offseason. Moon was traded to the Minnesota Vikings in the spring. Guard Mike Munchak announced his retirement in the summer. Defensive coordinator Buddy Ryan had already left the Oilers shortly after the end of the 1993 season. He became the head coach and general manager of the Arizona Cardinals.

Those changes immediately affected the Oilers in 1994. Houston was the lowest-scoring team in the NFL. Even with a win over the Jets in the season finale, the Oilers dropped all the way to a league-worst 2–14. Their time among the NFL's elite was over.

Before the 1995 season started, newspaper reports in Tennessee said Nashville mayor Phil Bredesen had been meeting with Oilers management. Owner Bud Adams had wanted the city of Houston to help pay for a new stadium for his team. He believed that the Astrodome was not modern enough. It did not appear that he would get his wish in Houston. Adams began looking for a city that would build a stadium for him.

Back on the field, defensive coordinator Jeff Fisher took over as head coach when Jack Pardee was fired with six games left in the 1994 season. He began making progress immediately, improving the team's record to 7–9 in 1995.

Meanwhile, the Oilers took their first step away from Houston. Nashville was willing to build them a stadium, and

Oilers quarterback Steve McNair runs onto the field during the team's first game in Tennessee in August 1997.

Adams and Bredesen signed a contract on November 16, 1995. The team planned to move to Tennessee in 1998.

But it turned out the Oilers would play just one more season in Houston. Knowing their team was leaving, Houston

Fans pack Adelphia Coliseum on August 27, 1999, for its first game, an exhibition between the Titans and Atlanta Falcons.

fans largely stayed away from the Astrodome in 1996. The Oilers went 6–2 on the road but just 2–6 at home. Adams was fed up and moved the team a year early. In June 1997, the Oilers left the only city they had ever known.

It became uncertain where the Tennessee Oilers would play their 1997 season. Groundbreaking ceremonies on the new stadium in Nashville did not take place until May 3, 1997. It was far too late for the stadium to be built for that fall. The team agreed to play the 1997 season at the Liberty Bowl in Memphis, Tennessee, a three-hour drive from Nashville.

The Oilers struggled to sell tickets in Memphis. Fans knew the team was there only temporarily. Few were willing to turn out to support Nashville's team. The largest crowd of the season was nearly 51,000 fans for the Pittsburgh game. But most of them were cheering for the Steelers. The Oilers finished 8–8 and left Memphis after one year.

But their new stadium was not ready yet. Instead, the team played the 1998 season at Vanderbilt University in Nashville. In response to feedback from Tennessee fans, Adams also announced that he would change the team's nickname. Oil was a major part of the Houston economy. But it had no meaning in Tennessee.

The team earned its first win in Nashville on October 18, 1998. It rolled over the Cincinnati Bengals 44–14. Before a third straight 8–8 season could be completed, Adams announced that the team would be changing its name to the Tennessee Titans for the 1999 season. Another new chapter in team history was about to be written.

AIR McNAIR

Steve McNair was the last quarterback drafted by the Houston Oilers. He was chosen with the team's first draft pick in 1995. He followed the team to Tennessee, where he became one of the best quarterbacks in franchise history. His 27,141 passing yards were second only to Warren Moon. He also was effective with his legs and racked up 3,439 rushing yards. He started the first Super Bowl in team history in 2000. He retired from the NFL in 2007. Tragically, he was killed in a domestic dispute in 2009.

CHAPTER 5

TO THE BASEMENT AND BACK

The Titans' new stadium, Adelphia Coliseum, was good to them in 1999. They finally had a home that was all theirs. The Titans went 8–0 at home. The 13–3 overall record was the best in franchise history.

The Titans won the "Music City Miracle" playoff game over Buffalo, then two more postseason games. Those three victories put the Titans in the Super Bowl for the first time in team history. But Tennessee lost 23–16 to the St. Louis Rams.

In 2000 Tennessee went 13–3 again and won the AFC Central Division title. The Titans' defense ranked first in the NFL. Running back Eddie George had the best season of his career with 1,509 rushing yards and 14 touchdowns.

Quarterback Steve McNair looks to pass against the Oakland Raiders.

TITANS
9

However, the Baltimore Ravens eliminated the host Titans 24–10 in the divisional playoff round.

After slipping to 7–9 in 2001, the Titans bounced back. The 2002 team started 1–4 but won 10 of its final 11 to extend its season. A 34–31 overtime home win over the Pittsburgh Steelers was followed by a 41–24 loss to the host Oakland Raiders in the AFC Championship Game.

NEW NAME

The Tennessee Oilers struggled at first to connect with fans in their new home. One way owner Bud Adams chose to help connect the team to Tennessee was with a new name. Adams put together a council of experts on Tennessee in 1998. They chose Titans out of a list of 39 finalists. Adams wanted a name that symbolized strength and heroism. And Nashville's nickname is "Athens of the South." The Titans were creatures from Greek mythology.

Titans quarterback Steve McNair shared the 2003 NFL MVP Award with Indianapolis Colts quarterback Peyton Manning. McNair led the Titans into the playoffs by throwing 24 touchdown passes. After beating the Ravens 20–17 in Baltimore in the wild-card round, the Titans were stopped in chilly New England. A late field goal gave the Patriots a 17–14 win.

George was released after the season; his 10,009 rushing yards were the most in team history. The team also parted ways with standout defensive end Jevon Kearse and "Music City Miracle" hero Frank Wycheck. Coupled with injuries to McNair, the Titans struggled and won just nine games the next two seasons.

The team pinned its hopes on quarterback Vince Young in the 2006 NFL Draft. Like McNair, Young was seen as both an effective passer and runner. The Titans chose Young third overall. He was inconsistent as a rookie and threw more interceptions than touchdown passes. Young put together a couple decent seasons but never established himself as a franchise quarterback. His play was inconsistent, and he struggled with injuries. After five seasons, Young was gone.

One constant through the ups and downs was head coach Jeff Fisher. He was far and away the winningest coach in team history. But after 16 seasons and 262 games, the Titans fired Fisher in January 2011.

Tennessee promoted Oilers legend Mike Munchak to head coach. Munchak had been an assistant coach with the team since 1994. The Titans also tried several new quarterbacks, including veterans Matt Hasselbeck and Ryan Fitzpatrick and first-round draft pick Jake Locker. None of them could put the Titans on top. Munchak lasted three seasons as head coach.

Marcus Mariota arrived in 2015 to give the Titans offense a new leader.

That was twice as long as Ken Whisenhunt, who replaced him and promptly went 3–20 in a season and a half.

After a 2–14 record in 2014, the Titans used their high draft pick in 2015 to try another quarterback. Marcus Mariota had won the Heisman Trophy at Oregon. Tennessee chose him second overall.

Mariota was thrust into action almost immediately. He started 12 games in 2015, throwing 19 touchdown passes and 10 interceptions. He went just 3–9 as a starter, but there was reason for hope. Mariota improved all those numbers in 2016, leading the Titans to a 9–7 record but coming up just short of the playoffs.

But 9–7 was good enough for the Titans to get into the postseason in 2017. Mariota's numbers declined, but the Titans did just enough to get back to the playoffs as a wild card. Mariota threw two second-half touchdown passes, and running back Derrick Henry also scored as the Titans won their first playoff game in 14 years, 22–21 at Kansas City. However, they fell to the Patriots the next week.

After finishing in the bottom half of the league in points allowed every year since 2012, the Titans needed to emphasize defense. In January 2018 they hired a new head coach, former NFL linebacker Mike Vrabel. He had played linebacker in the NFL for 14 seasons. But he had never been a head coach before. In Vrabel's first season, the Titans finished 9–7 but lost to Indianapolis in the final week to miss the playoffs by one game. Still, a young head coach and a top young quarterback can be a recipe for success in the NFL. Titans fans hoped that recipe would lead to a Super Bowl.

TIMELINE

1960
The Houston Oilers begin play in the American Football League (AFL).

1961
The Oilers win the first AFL Championship Game on January 1, beating the Chargers 24–16.

1961
Houston wins its second AFL title on December 24, topping the Chargers 10–3.

1962
Houston misses out on a possible third straight title when it falls to the Dallas Texans 20–17 in double overtime on December 23.

1970
The Oilers and nine other AFL franchises merge into the NFL.

1978
The Oilers draft future Hall of Fame running back Earl Campbell.

1978
The Oilers reach the playoffs for the first time as an NFL member.

1980
A crowd of 70,000 greets the Oilers after they lose to the Steelers in Pittsburgh in the AFC Championship Game on January 6.

1987
Houston lands the first of seven straight playoff berths.

1995
The Oilers reach an agreement on November 16 to move to Nashville, Tennessee.

1996 — The Oilers play their last game in Houston. They lose 21–13 to the Cincinnati Bengals on December 15.

1997 — The team relocates temporarily to Memphis, playing one season at the Liberty Bowl.

1998 — Vanderbilt University in Nashville provides the team's temporary home stadium.

1999 — The team moves into the new Adelphia Coliseum and changes its name to the Tennessee Titans.

2000 — The "Music City Miracle" extends the team's first season as the Titans on January 8.

2000 — The Titans reach their first Super Bowl but lose to the St. Louis Rams 23–16.

2009 — The Titans' Chris Johnson becomes the sixth player in NFL history to rush for 2,000 yards in a season.

2015 — The Titans draft Oregon quarterback Marcus Mariota with the second overall pick.

2018 — On January 6, Mariota leads the team to a comeback victory over the Kansas City Chiefs for its first playoff win in 14 years.

2018 — Derrick Henry ties an NFL record with a 99-yard touchdown run against Jacksonville on December 6.

QUICK STATS

FRANCHISE HISTORY

Houston Oilers (1960–96)
Tennessee Oilers (1997–98)
Tennessee Titans (1999–)

SUPER BOWLS *(wins in bold)*

1999 (XXXIV)

AFL CHAMPIONSHIP GAMES *(1960–69, wins in bold)*

1960, **1961**, 1962

DIVISION CHAMPIONSHIPS *(since 1970 AFL-NFL merger)*

1991, 1993, 2000, 2002, 2008

KEY COACHES

Jeff Fisher (1994–2010): 142–120, 5–6 (playoffs)
O. A. "Bum" Phillips (1975–80): 55–35, 4–3 (playoffs)

KEY PLAYERS *(position, seasons with team)*

Elvin Bethea (DE, 1968–83)
George Blanda (QB/K, 1960–66)
Earl Campbell (RB, 1978–84)
Eddie George (RB, 1996–2003)
Ernest Givins (WR, 1986–94)
Charley Hennigan (WR, 1960–66)
Ken Houston (S, 1967–72)
Marcus Mariota (QB, 2015–)
Bruce Matthews (G/C/T, 1983–2001)
Steve McNair (QB, 1995–2005)
Warren Moon (QB, 1984–93)
Mike Munchak (G, 1982–93)
Dan Pastorini (QB, 1971–79)

HOME FIELDS

Nissan Stadium (1999–)
Also known as Adelphia Coliseum, The Coliseum, and LP Field
Vanderbilt Stadium (1998)
Liberty Bowl (1997)
Houston Astrodome (1968–96)
Rice Stadium (1965–67)
Jeppesen Stadium (1960–64)

*All statistics through 2018 season

QUOTES AND ANECDOTES

Through the 2018 season, the Oilers/Titans had retired six uniform numbers: Warren Moon (1), Earl Campbell (34), Jim Norton (43), Mike Munchak (63), Elvin Bethea (65), and Bruce Matthews (74).

The Titans and Oilers had worn white helmets ever since 1975. In 2018 the team introduced new uniforms that included navy blue helmets. The Titans kept the same color scheme and logo, but the uniforms had new designs. The new uniforms were created to celebrate the team's 20th anniversary in Tennessee.

Through 2018 Warren Moon was the franchise leader in passing yards with 33,685. Eddie George led in rushing yards with 10,009. Ernest Givins led in receiving yards with 7,935.

Warren Moon had a chance to set an NFL record in a late-season game in 1990. But he chose not to try adding to his 527 passing yards. The Oilers had a comfortable lead in a 27–10 win over the Kansas City Chiefs. Moon's total was the second highest in NFL history behind Norm Van Brocklin's 554 yards for the Los Angeles Rams in 1951 against the New York Yanks.

After the Oilers moved out, the Astrodome remained in use as the home of the Houston Astros baseball team until 1999. The building mostly sat empty in the 20 years afterward, but it was named to the National Register of Historic Places in 2014. Many different uses were discussed for the dome. In 2018 a $105 million renovation was approved to turn the Astrodome into a multipurpose event space.

GLOSSARY

contract
An agreement to play for a certain team.

coordinator
An assistant coach who is in charge of the offense or defense.

draft
A system that allows teams to acquire new players coming into a league.

franchise
A sports organization, including the top-level team and all minor league affiliates.

lateral
A pass that goes sideways or backward.

merge
Join with another to create something new, such as a company, a team, or a league.

playoffs
A set of games played after the regular season that decides which team is the champion.

rival
An opponent with whom a player or team has a fierce and ongoing competition.

rookie
A professional athlete in his or her first year of competition.

sack
A tackle of the quarterback behind the line of scrimmage before he can pass the ball.

strike
A work stoppage caused by a disagreement between labor and management.

MORE INFORMATION

BOOKS

Karras, Steven M. *Tennessee Titans*. New York: AV2 by Weigl, 2018.

Kortemeier, Todd. *Tennessee Titans*. Minneapolis, MN: Abdo Publishing, 2017.

Lajiness, Katie. *Tennessee Titans*. Minneapolis, MN: Abdo Publishing, 2017.

ONLINE RESOURCES

Booklinks
NONFICTION NETWORK
FREE! ONLINE NONFICTION RESOURCES

To learn more about the Tennessee Titans, visit **abdobooklinks.com** or scan this QR code. These links are routinely monitored and updated to provide the most current information available.

PLACE TO VISIT

Saint Thomas Sports Park
460 Great Circle Road
Nashville, TN 37228
615–565–4000
titansonline.com/about-us

The Titans team headquarters and practice facility is located just north of downtown Nashville. The team also holds training camp here.

INDEX

ABOUT THE AUTHOR

William Meier has worked as an author and editor in the publishing industry for more than 25 years. He resides in St. Louis, Missouri, with his wife and their poodle, Macy.